DIY

Bucket List

100+
- ✓ PRompts,
- ✓ Lists, &
- ✓ IDEAS

for Planning the Rest
—and BEST—of Your Life!

Molly Burford

Adams Media

New York   London   Toronto   Sydney   New Delhi

Adams Media
An Imprint of Simon & Schuster, Inc.
57 Littlefield Street
Avon, Massachusetts 02322

First Adams Media trade paperback edition January 2021

ADAMS MEDIA and colophon are trademarks of Simon & Schuster.

For information about special discounts for bulk purchases, please contact Simon & Schuster Special Sales at 1-866-506-1949 or business@simonandschuster.com.

The Simon & Schuster Speakers Bureau can bring authors to your live event. For more information or to book an event contact the Simon & Schuster Speakers Bureau at 1-866-248-3049 or visit our website at www.simonspeakers.com.

Interior design by Julia Jacintho
Interior illustrations and hand lettering by Priscilla Yuen

Manufactured in the United States of America

10 9 8 7 6 5 4 3 2 1

Library of Congress Cataloging-in-Publication Data has been applied for.

ISBN 978-1-5072-1561-6
ISBN 978-1-5072-1562-3 (ebook)

Contents

Introduction ... 6

PART 1
Writing Prompts ... 8

PART 2

Goals ... 40

PART 3

Big Dreams ... 62

Introduction

Life is truly a gift. It's overflowing with amazing possibilities, exciting potential, and endless wonders. You can grow and love and experience everything (and everyone) this wonderful planet has to offer—all you need to do is make specific, actionable plans. You need to identify whom and what you want to focus on and let go of all the rest. And that's what *DIY Bucket List* is for! A bucket list is a record of accomplishments and experiences you hope to achieve during your lifetime. This book will help you decide what—and who—is important to you and keep track of all of your goals.

DIY Bucket List serves as a guide on your journey to cross off every item. You'll find the following:

- **Dozens of writing prompts** to help you determine what's most important to you in all areas of your life. For example, you'll describe every glorious detail of your perfect getaway.

- **Checklists** to capture bucket list goals under the same category, like lists of movies to watch, books to read, shows to binge, sports to learn, and special meals to eat. Each item will have a priority rating so you can figure out what to do first.

- **Journaling pages** to record actionable bucket list goals based on what you figured out from the writing prompts. If you want to take an amazing vacation, when will you go? Who will go with you? How will you save up for it? After you check off each item, you'll find space to reflect on the experience. Was your vacation as amazing as you knew it would be? What exceeded your expectations? What do you want to be sure to remember?

We're all busy—but you can accomplish all of your bucket list goals when you're organized and thoughtful about how you track them. Whether that's being with your family, spending time with friends, finally getting on that plane to Italy, or writing a novel that's always been deep inside, *DIY Bucket List* will take your dreams from these pages into reality.

No matter where you are in your journey—be it your teens, twenties, midlife, or golden years—you can start living your life joyously. Fully. Completely. It starts with you. Be excited and curious about what's to come. Turn the page and let's start planning!

PART 1

Writing Prompts

What are the things that are most important to you? Is it your relationships? Is it pushing yourself educationally? Is it traveling around the earth to experience the wonders that can be found there? Maybe a combination of all of those things? That's up to you to find out in the next pages, with thirty prompts that will guide you to figure out what exactly is most important to you. They'll help stimulate your thinking; they'll push you to look at your life goals in a new way. And above all, they'll guide you toward creating your own bucket list, geared toward your needs and wishes. The items on that bucket list will go in the lists you compile in Part 2.

Be open-minded, curious, and honest in these answers, and don't automatically reject any of them. You might be surprised to learn what you value!

The Perfect Getaway

You wake up one day, and you're no longer in your bedroom. You're in a hotel. Where in the world would this hotel be? You get up from the bed and approach the window—what do you hope to see when you open the drapes? What scents would you want wafting up to you? Is the scene quiet or teeming with people? Write a brief description of your dream scenario.

_____

_____

_____

_____

_____

_____

_____

_____

_____

_____

_____

_____

_____

_____

_____

_____

_____

_____

_____

_____

Life's a Movie

If your life were a movie, what kind of genre would it be? Would it be action, full of adventure? Would it be a romantic comedy? Would you be the lead character or playing a supporting role? Write out a synopsis of your life movie here.

No Regrets!

What is something you regret missing? How can you make up for it? What experiences can you seek out that could replicate the feelings you missed the first time around?

How Do You Role?

How could you be your own role model? What actions can you take to lead a life you're proud of? Is it running a 5K? Entering an art show? Writing your novel? Getting that promotion you've been working so hard for? Don't be afraid to dream big!

What's Your Experience Style?

Would you rather be surprised or prepared? Ecstatic or content? Why? Your answers can help you decide the types of adventures you'd like to experience and how to create them.

Who Are Your People?

What relationships are most important to you? List your five most important relationships and why they mean so much to you. How do you like to spend time with these people?

The Perfect Weekend

It's Friday afternoon before a perfect weekend. What does that perfect weekend look like to you? What will you do? Is it going to be productive? Full of socializing? List everything you will (or won't!) do during this coming weekend.

Work It Out

It's been said if you do what you love, you'll never work a day in your life. If this is true, what do you love to do? Creative feats? Helping others? Solving puzzles? Brainstorm here and think of ways you can implement what you love doing into your work life.

Make the Most of Everyday

You've thought about the perfect getaway and the perfect weekend. But what would a day in your perfect everyday life look like? Where would you be working? What would you eat for your meals? What hobbies would you make time for? Who would you see?

Notice Your Distractions

Distraction is natural, but it takes away from the present moment—
your life. What are some ways you distract yourself? Is it mindless
streaming services? Online shopping for things you really don't need?
Figure out what distracts you and list it. Then write out some ideas for
how to substitute those behaviors with more productive, present ones.

Whom Would You Like to Meet in the Mirror?

It's ten years from now. You go to the bathroom to get ready for the day. As you're reaching for your toothbrush, you look in the mirror. Whom do you see? What has that person accomplished? What do they still want to do? What traits would you use to describe this person?

Seek New Experiences over Comforting Familiarity

While comfort is totally necessary at times, it's also not the only way to feel content. Seeking new experiences awakens the senses and enlivens the spirit. Whether it's trying a new cuisine, traveling to a place you've never been, going on a date with someone who isn't necessarily your type, there are plenty of ways to embrace novelty. What are some ways you could implement the new into your own life? Write it out here. Oh, and be bold with your ideas. Skydiving is totally on the table, if that's your thing.

Stranded Island Dreamin'

You're stranded on a desert island. How would you make the most of it? What would your days look like? Whom would you want stranded with you? What music would you play? How would you do without technology? What would you miss about home? Dream up this scenario.

Child's Play

What did you love to do as a kid? Were you an avid reader? Did you love getting your hands dirty outside? Did you play pretend? What about sports? Think back and then think to now and how you could implement those activities into adulthood.

Life's a Party

It's a miracle you're here, and just being alive is something worth celebrating! Instead of waiting for summer, a wedding, a promotion, or the weekend to celebrate, why not find a way to turn the simple act of living into a party? What are some little victories you can think of today that deserve a glass of champagne? Everything counts. List it here.

And the Lottery Winner Is...

You just won the lottery. Congratulations! What will you do with your newfound wealth? How will you share it? Will you still work? What will you do for yourself with that cash? The way you answer will tell you a lot about what and whom you value.

A Fresh Start

If you got the chance to start your life over, would you? Why or why not? To expand on this question, are there good experiences you wouldn't want to let go? Or more difficult times that still taught you a lot that you wouldn't want to give up? Or would you rather not have gone through certain things at all? Be honest and curious!

_____

_____

_____

_____

_____

_____

_____

_____

_____

_____

_____

_____

_____

_____

_____

_____

_____

_____

_____

_____

_____

Lose Yourself

Sometimes, time gets away from us because we are so busy living and enjoying the present moment. What are you doing when you notice this happening to you? Are you writing? Drawing? Playing cards with friends? Painting? Reading?

Whose Life Do You Admire?

Think about anyone in your life (or those you don't know personally) and think about the life they live. What do you admire about it? What parts would you like to have for your own life? And what parts would you *not* want?

When Was the Last Time You Felt Joyful?

We're talking over the moon and gleeful. Where were you? Whom were you with? What were you doing? How can you implement more moments like these into your life?

_____

_____

_____

_____

_____

_____

_____

_____

_____

_____

_____

_____

_____

_____

_____

_____

_____

_____

_____

What Both Scares You and Excites You?

Is it getting your dream job? Finding your life partner? Going for a goal that would completely change your life even though there would be sacrifice involved?

It's the End of Your Life. Describe the Life You Lived

Adventurous? Meaningful? Loving? Carefree? Full? Think of your ideal adjectives and list them here. Then think about ways to cultivate them!

Time Out

You've developed the ability to stop time. Pretty cool. But you can only use it five times in your life. What moments would you want to pause and savor? Your wedding? The birth of a child? Getting your PhD? Calling your grandma? Why these moments?

Speak Another Language

If you could speak another language, which one would it be, and why? Whom would you talk to? Would you go to another country to speak that language? List five books written in that language that you would read.

What Looks Good to You?

The person whose opinion matters most in your life is you. It's easy to get wrapped up in others' thoughts about what you should be doing, but when it comes down to it, they aren't living your life; you are. Taking everyone else out of the equation, if you were to have infinite approval no matter what, what would your life look like?

Who (or What) Makes You Forget Your Phone?

Do you have a bad habit of constantly checking your phone? Most people do! Now think about this: When are the moments you notice you don't reach for your phone? Whom are you with? What are you doing? How can you make more room for experiences like that?

Troublemakers

What's something you would do if you couldn't get into trouble? Would you break into the Louvre at night to miss the crowds? Run through the airport to tell someone you love them, even though you didn't buy a ticket? Stay up until dawn even if you had work the next day? Sometimes, breaking the rules is part of the fun! Figure out what that looks like to you.

Food's Up!

You can only eat one type of cuisine for the rest of your life. What is it? How can you integrate it more fully into the meals you're eating now?

You're Booked!

You just joined a book club, and you get to choose the first book. What do you choose? Why?

The Art of Success

If you were to achieve success in any artistic field, what would it be? How would your success be defined? Would you become rich for success, or does that not matter? Write a short paragraph describing your progression from artistic obscurity to fame.

PART 2

Goals

Now that you've figured out what is important to you, it's time to get even *more* specific. In this part, you're going to list a number of different goals you want to fulfill. Under "Priority," there's a place to rank each goal from 1 to 5, with 1 being lowest priority and 5 being highest. For some categories there's a space to write details on how you want to enjoy the experience. For example, if you've always wanted to try escargot, do you want to prepare that dish yourself at home or enjoy it at a favorite restaurant, or is your goal to dine on this classic dish in Paris? If there's a musical you want to experience, is it Broadway or bust, or would a local production do? It's your life— you decide how you want to live it!

Do you want to donate to causes you care about? What about doing a flash mob? Make the list, and check it off as you succeed!

There are plenty of skills to master during your lifetime and plenty of time to do so! Don't be afraid to reach for the stars!

Books to Read

Name of Book:

_____

Author:

_____

Priority (1–5): ✳ ✳ ✳ ✳ ✳
Accomplished! Date:_____

Name of Book:

_____

Author:

_____

Priority (1–5): ✳ ✳ ✳ ✳ ✳
Accomplished! Date:_____

Name of Book:

_____

Author:

_____

Priority (1–5): ✳ ✳ ✳ ✳ ✳
Accomplished! Date:_____

Name of Book:

_____

Author:

_____

Priority (1–5): ✳ ✳ ✳ ✳ ✳
Accomplished! Date:_____

Name of Book:

_____

Author:

_____

Priority (1–5): ✳ ✳ ✳ ✳ ✳
Accomplished! Date:_____

Name of Book:

_____

Author:

_____

Priority (1–5): ✳ ✳ ✳ ✳ ✳
Accomplished! Date:_____

Name of Book:

_____

Author:

_____

Priority (1–5): ✳ ✳ ✳ ✳ ✳
Accomplished! Date:_____

Name of Book:

_____

Author:

_____

Priority (1–5): ✳ ✳ ✳ ✳ ✳
Accomplished! Date:_____

Movies to See

Movie:
_____

Venue/Platform:
_____

Priority (1–5): ✳ ✳ ✳ ✳ ✳
Accomplished! Date:_____

Movie:
_____

Venue/Platform:
_____

Priority (1–5): ✳ ✳ ✳ ✳ ✳
Accomplished! Date:_____

Movie:
_____

Venue/Platform:
_____

Priority (1–5): ✳ ✳ ✳ ✳ ✳
Accomplished! Date:_____

Movie:
_____

Venue/Platform:
_____

Priority (1–5): ✳ ✳ ✳ ✳ ✳
Accomplished! Date:_____

Movie:
_____

Venue/Platform:
_____

Priority (1–5): ✳ ✳ ✳ ✳ ✳
Accomplished! Date:_____

Movie:
_____

Venue/Platform:
_____

Priority (1–5): ✳ ✳ ✳ ✳ ✳
Accomplished! Date:_____

Movie:
_____

Venue/Platform:
_____

Priority (1–5): ✳ ✳ ✳ ✳ ✳
Accomplished! Date:_____

Movie:
_____

Venue/Platform:
_____

Priority (1–5): ✳ ✳ ✳ ✳ ✳
Accomplished! Date:_____

Shows to Binge

Show:
_____

Venue/Platform:
_____

Priority (1–5): ✳ ✳ ✳ ✳ ✳
Accomplished! Date:_____

Show:
_____

Venue/Platform:
_____

Priority (1–5): ✳ ✳ ✳ ✳ ✳
Accomplished! Date:_____

Show:
_____

Venue/Platform:
_____

Priority (1–5): ✳ ✳ ✳ ✳ ✳
Accomplished! Date:_____

Show:
_____

Venue/Platform:
_____

Priority (1–5): ✳ ✳ ✳ ✳ ✳
Accomplished! Date:_____

Show:
_____

Venue/Platform:
_____

Priority (1–5): ✳ ✳ ✳ ✳ ✳
Accomplished! Date:_____

Show:
_____

Venue/Platform:
_____

Priority (1–5): ✳ ✳ ✳ ✳ ✳
Accomplished! Date:_____

Show:
_____

Venue/Platform:
_____

Priority (1–5): ✳ ✳ ✳ ✳ ✳
Accomplished! Date:_____

Show:
_____

Venue/Platform:
_____

Priority (1–5): ✳ ✳ ✳ ✳ ✳
Accomplished! Date:_____

Gastronomic Experiences to Savor

Culinary Experience:

_____

_____

Where/How to Enjoy It:

_____

_____

Priority (1–5): ✳ ✳ ✳ ✳ ✳

Accomplished! Date:_____

Culinary Experience:

_____

_____

Where/How to Enjoy It:

_____

_____

Priority (1–5): ✳ ✳ ✳ ✳ ✳

Accomplished! Date:_____

Culinary Experience:

_____

_____

Where/How to Enjoy It:

_____

_____

Priority (1–5): ✳ ✳ ✳ ✳ ✳

Accomplished! Date:_____

Culinary Experience:

_____

_____

Where/How to Enjoy It:

_____

_____

Priority (1–5): ✳ ✳ ✳ ✳ ✳

Accomplished! Date:_____

Culinary Experience:

_____

_____

Where/How to Enjoy It:

_____

_____

Priority (1–5): ✳ ✳ ✳ ✳ ✳

Accomplished! Date:_____

Culinary Experience:

_____

_____

Where/How to Enjoy It:

_____

_____

Priority (1–5): ✳ ✳ ✳ ✳ ✳

Accomplished! Date:_____

Good Works to Perform

Cause/Charity/Person in Need:

_____

Action to Take:

_____

_____

_____

Priority (1–5): ✳ ✳ ✳ ✳ ✳

Accomplished! Date:_____

Cause/Charity/Person in Need:

_____

Action to Take:

_____

_____

_____

Priority (1–5): ✳ ✳ ✳ ✳ ✳

Accomplished! Date:_____

Cause/Charity/Person in Need:

_____

Action to Take:

_____

_____

_____

Priority (1–5): ✳ ✳ ✳ ✳ ✳

Accomplished! Date:_____

Cause/Charity/Person in Need:

_____

Action to Take:

_____

_____

_____

Priority (1–5): ✳ ✳ ✳ ✳ ✳

Accomplished! Date:_____

Cause/Charity/Person in Need:

_____

Action to Take:

_____

_____

_____

Priority (1–5): ✳ ✳ ✳ ✳ ✳

Accomplished! Date:_____

Cause/Charity/Person in Need:

_____

Action to Take:

_____

_____

_____

Priority (1–5): ✳ ✳ ✳ ✳ ✳

Accomplished! Date:_____

Historic Places to Visit

Name of Site:

Location:

Priority (1–5): ✳ ✳ ✳ ✳ ✳
Accomplished! Date: _____

Name of Site:

Location:

Priority (1–5): ✳ ✳ ✳ ✳ ✳
Accomplished! Date: _____

Name of Site:

Location:

Priority (1–5): ✳ ✳ ✳ ✳ ✳
Accomplished! Date: _____

Name of Site:

Location:

Priority (1–5): ✳ ✳ ✳ ✳ ✳
Accomplished! Date: _____

Name of Site:

Location:

Priority (1–5): ✳ ✳ ✳ ✳ ✳
Accomplished! Date: _____

Name of Site:

Location:

Priority (1–5): ✳ ✳ ✳ ✳ ✳
Accomplished! Date: _____

Name of Site:

Location:

Priority (1–5): ✳ ✳ ✳ ✳ ✳
Accomplished! Date: _____

Name of Site:

Location:

Priority (1–5): ✳ ✳ ✳ ✳ ✳
Accomplished! Date: _____

Museums to Visit

Name of Museum:

_____

Key Exhibition:

_____

Priority (1–5): ✲ ✲ ✲ ✲ ✲
Accomplished! Date:_____

Name of Museum:

_____

Key Exhibition:

_____

Priority (1–5): ✲ ✲ ✲ ✲ ✲
Accomplished! Date:_____

Name of Museum:

_____

Key Exhibition:

_____

Priority (1–5): ✲ ✲ ✲ ✲ ✲
Accomplished! Date:_____

Name of Museum:

_____

Key Exhibition:

_____

Priority (1–5): ✲ ✲ ✲ ✲ ✲
Accomplished! Date:_____

Name of Museum:

_____

Key Exhibition:

_____

Priority (1–5): ✲ ✲ ✲ ✲ ✲
Accomplished! Date:_____

Name of Museum:

_____

Key Exhibition:

_____

Priority (1–5): ✲ ✲ ✲ ✲ ✲
Accomplished! Date:_____

Name of Museum:

_____

Key Exhibition:

_____

Priority (1–5): ✲ ✲ ✲ ✲ ✲
Accomplished! Date:_____

Name of Museum:

_____

Key Exhibition:

_____

Priority (1–5): ✲ ✲ ✲ ✲ ✲
Accomplished! Date:_____

Letters to Write

To Whom?

_____

Why?

_____

Priority (1–5): ✳ ✳ ✳ ✳ ✳
Accomplished! Date:_____

To Whom?

_____

Why?

_____

Priority (1–5): ✳ ✳ ✳ ✳ ✳
Accomplished! Date:_____

To Whom?

_____

Why?

_____

Priority (1–5): ✳ ✳ ✳ ✳ ✳
Accomplished! Date:_____

To Whom?

_____

Why?

_____

Priority (1–5): ✳ ✳ ✳ ✳ ✳
Accomplished! Date:_____

To Whom?

_____

Why?

_____

Priority (1–5): ✳ ✳ ✳ ✳ ✳
Accomplished! Date:_____

To Whom?

_____

Why?

_____

Priority (1–5): ✳ ✳ ✳ ✳ ✳
Accomplished! Date:_____

To Whom?

_____

Why?

_____

Priority (1–5): ✳ ✳ ✳ ✳ ✳
Accomplished! Date:_____

To Whom?

_____

Why?

_____

Priority (1–5): ✳ ✳ ✳ ✳ ✳
Accomplished! Date:_____

Cities to Visit

Name of City:

_____

Distance from Home:

_____

Priority (1–5): ✳ ✳ ✳ ✳ ✳

Accomplished! Date: _____

Name of City:

_____

Distance from Home:

_____

Priority (1–5): ✳ ✳ ✳ ✳ ✳

Accomplished! Date: _____

Name of City:

_____

Distance from Home:

_____

Priority (1–5): ✳ ✳ ✳ ✳ ✳

Accomplished! Date: _____

Name of City:

_____

Distance from Home:

_____

Priority (1–5): ✳ ✳ ✳ ✳ ✳

Accomplished! Date: _____

Name of City:

_____

Distance from Home:

_____

Priority (1–5): ✳ ✳ ✳ ✳ ✳

Accomplished! Date: _____

Name of City:

_____

Distance from Home:

_____

Priority (1–5): ✳ ✳ ✳ ✳ ✳

Accomplished! Date: _____

Name of City:

_____

Distance from Home:

_____

Priority (1–5): ✳ ✳ ✳ ✳ ✳

Accomplished! Date: _____

Name of City:

_____

Distance from Home:

_____

Priority (1–5): ✳ ✳ ✳ ✳ ✳

Accomplished! Date: _____

Drinks to Try

Drink Name:

_____

Where to Imbibe:

_____

Priority (1–5): ★ ★ ★ ★ ★

Accomplished! Date: _____

Drink Name:

_____

Where to Imbibe:

_____

Priority (1–5): ★ ★ ★ ★ ★

Accomplished! Date: _____

Drink Name:

_____

Where to Imbibe:

_____

Priority (1–5): ★ ★ ★ ★ ★

Accomplished! Date: _____

Drink Name:

_____

Where to Imbibe:

_____

Priority (1–5): ★ ★ ★ ★ ★

Accomplished! Date: _____

Drink Name:

_____

Where to Imbibe:

_____

Priority (1–5): ★ ★ ★ ★ ★

Accomplished! Date: _____

Drink Name:

_____

Where to Imbibe:

_____

Priority (1–5): ★ ★ ★ ★ ★

Accomplished! Date: _____

Drink Name:

_____

Where to Imbibe:

_____

Priority (1–5): ★ ★ ★ ★ ★

Accomplished! Date: _____

Drink Name:

_____

Where to Imbibe:

_____

Priority (1–5): ★ ★ ★ ★ ★

Accomplished! Date: _____

Local Landmarks to Explore

Landmark Name:

_____

Distance from Home:

_____

Priority (1–5): ✳ ✳ ✳ ✳ ✳
Accomplished! Date:_____

Landmark Name:

_____

Distance from Home:

_____

Priority (1–5): ✳ ✳ ✳ ✳ ✳
Accomplished! Date:_____

Landmark Name:

_____

Distance from Home:

_____

Priority (1–5): ✳ ✳ ✳ ✳ ✳
Accomplished! Date:_____

Landmark Name:

_____

Distance from Home:

_____

Priority (1–5): ✳ ✳ ✳ ✳ ✳
Accomplished! Date:_____

Landmark Name:

_____

Distance from Home:

_____

Priority (1–5): ✳ ✳ ✳ ✳ ✳
Accomplished! Date:_____

Landmark Name:

_____

Distance from Home:

_____

Priority (1–5): ✳ ✳ ✳ ✳ ✳
Accomplished! Date:_____

Landmark Name:

_____

Distance from Home:

_____

Priority (1–5): ✳ ✳ ✳ ✳ ✳
Accomplished! Date:_____

Landmark Name:

_____

Distance from Home:

_____

Priority (1–5): ✳ ✳ ✳ ✳ ✳
Accomplished! Date:_____

Beaches to Lie On

Beach Name:

_____

Location:

_____

Priority (1–5): ✳ ✳ ✳ ✳ ✳
Accomplished! Date:_____

Beach Name:

_____

Location:

_____

Priority (1–5): ✳ ✳ ✳ ✳ ✳
Accomplished! Date:_____

Beach Name:

_____

Location:

_____

Priority (1–5): ✳ ✳ ✳ ✳ ✳
Accomplished! Date:_____

Beach Name:

_____

Location:

_____

Priority (1–5): ✳ ✳ ✳ ✳ ✳
Accomplished! Date:_____

Beach Name:

_____

Location:

_____

Priority (1–5): ✳ ✳ ✳ ✳ ✳
Accomplished! Date:_____

Beach Name:

_____

Location:

_____

Priority (1–5): ✳ ✳ ✳ ✳ ✳
Accomplished! Date:_____

Beach Name:

_____

Location:

_____

Priority (1–5): ✳ ✳ ✳ ✳ ✳
Accomplished! Date:_____

Beach Name:

_____

Location:

_____

Priority (1–5): ✳ ✳ ✳ ✳ ✳
Accomplished! Date:_____

Hikes to Take

Trail Name:

_____

Length of Trail:

_____

Priority (1–5): ✳ ✳ ✳ ✳ ✳

Accomplished! Date: _____

Trail Name:

_____

Length of Trail:

_____

Priority (1–5): ✳ ✳ ✳ ✳ ✳

Accomplished! Date: _____

Trail Name:

_____

Length of Trail:

_____

Priority (1–5): ✳ ✳ ✳ ✳ ✳

Accomplished! Date: _____

Trail Name:

_____

Length of Trail:

_____

Priority (1–5): ✳ ✳ ✳ ✳ ✳

Accomplished! Date: _____

Trail Name:

_____

Length of Trail:

_____

Priority (1–5): ✳ ✳ ✳ ✳ ✳

Accomplished! Date: _____

Trail Name:

_____

Length of Trail:

_____

Priority (1–5): ✳ ✳ ✳ ✳ ✳

Accomplished! Date: _____

Trail Name:

_____

Length of Trail:

_____

Priority (1–5): ✳ ✳ ✳ ✳ ✳

Accomplished! Date: _____

Trail Name:

_____

Length of Trail:

_____

Priority (1–5): ✳ ✳ ✳ ✳ ✳

Accomplished! Date: _____

Animals to See

Animal:

Where to See It:

Priority (1–5): ✻ ✻ ✻ ✻ ✻

Accomplished! Date:_____

Animal:

Where to See It:

Priority (1–5): ✻ ✻ ✻ ✻ ✻

Accomplished! Date:_____

Animal:

Where to See It:

Priority (1–5): ✻ ✻ ✻ ✻ ✻

Accomplished! Date:_____

Animal:

Where to See It:

Priority (1–5): ✻ ✻ ✻ ✻ ✻

Accomplished! Date:_____

Animal:

Where to See It:

Priority (1–5): ✻ ✻ ✻ ✻ ✻

Accomplished! Date:_____

Animal:

Where to See It:

Priority (1–5): ✻ ✻ ✻ ✻ ✻

Accomplished! Date:_____

Animal:

Where to See It:

Priority (1–5): ✻ ✻ ✻ ✻ ✻

Accomplished! Date:_____

Animal:

Where to See It:

Priority (1–5): ✻ ✻ ✻ ✻ ✻

Accomplished! Date:_____

New Hobbies to Try

Hobby:

_____

Equipment Needed:

_____

_____

Priority (1–5): ✳ ✳ ✳ ✳ ✳
Accomplished! Date:_____

Hobby:

_____

Equipment Needed:

_____

_____

Priority (1–5): ✳ ✳ ✳ ✳ ✳
Accomplished! Date:_____

Hobby:

_____

Equipment Needed:

_____

_____

Priority (1–5): ✳ ✳ ✳ ✳ ✳
Accomplished! Date:_____

Hobby:

_____

Equipment Needed:

_____

_____

Priority (1–5): ✳ ✳ ✳ ✳ ✳
Accomplished! Date:_____

Hobby:

_____

Equipment Needed:

_____

_____

Priority (1–5): ✳ ✳ ✳ ✳ ✳
Accomplished! Date:_____

Hobby:

_____

Equipment Needed:

_____

_____

Priority (1–5): ✳ ✳ ✳ ✳ ✳
Accomplished! Date:_____

Skills to Master

Skill:

_____

_____

Where to Learn It:

_____

_____

Priority (1–5): ✷ ✷ ✷ ✷ ✷

Accomplished! Date: _____

Skill:

_____

_____

Where to Learn It:

_____

_____

Priority (1–5): ✷ ✷ ✷ ✷ ✷

Accomplished! Date: _____

Skill:

_____

_____

Where to Learn It:

_____

_____

Priority (1–5): ✷ ✷ ✷ ✷ ✷

Accomplished! Date: _____

Skill:

_____

_____

Where to Learn It:

_____

_____

Priority (1–5): ✷ ✷ ✷ ✷ ✷

Accomplished! Date: _____

Skill:

_____

_____

Where to Learn It:

_____

_____

Priority (1–5): ✷ ✷ ✷ ✷ ✷

Accomplished! Date: _____

Skill:

_____

_____

Where to Learn It:

_____

_____

Priority (1–5): ✷ ✷ ✷ ✷ ✷

Accomplished! Date: _____

Fears to Conquer

Personal Fear:

_____

_____

How to Beat It:

_____

_____

Priority (1–5): ✶ ✶ ✶ ✶ ✶

Accomplished! Date:_____

Personal Fear:

_____

_____

How to Beat It:

_____

_____

Priority (1–5): ✶ ✶ ✶ ✶ ✶

Accomplished! Date:_____

Personal Fear:

_____

_____

How to Beat It:

_____

_____

Priority (1–5): ✶ ✶ ✶ ✶ ✶

Accomplished! Date:_____

Personal Fear:

_____

_____

How to Beat It:

_____

_____

Priority (1–5): ✶ ✶ ✶ ✶ ✶

Accomplished! Date:_____

Personal Fear:

_____

_____

How to Beat It:

_____

_____

Priority (1–5): ✶ ✶ ✶ ✶ ✶

Accomplished! Date:_____

Personal Fear:

_____

_____

How to Beat It:

_____

_____

Priority (1–5): ✶ ✶ ✶ ✶ ✶

Accomplished! Date:_____

Home Improvements to Make

Type of Renovation:

_____

_____

DIY or Hire Out?

_____

_____

Priority (1–5): ✳ ✳ ✳ ✳ ✳

Accomplished! Date:_____

Type of Renovation:

_____

_____

DIY or Hire Out?

_____

_____

Priority (1–5): ✳ ✳ ✳ ✳ ✳

Accomplished! Date:_____

Type of Renovation:

_____

_____

DIY or Hire Out?

_____

_____

Priority (1–5): ✳ ✳ ✳ ✳ ✳

Accomplished! Date:_____

Type of Renovation:

_____

_____

DIY or Hire Out?

_____

_____

Priority (1–5): ✳ ✳ ✳ ✳ ✳

Accomplished! Date:_____

Type of Renovation:

_____

_____

DIY or Hire Out?

_____

_____

Priority (1–5): ✳ ✳ ✳ ✳ ✳

Accomplished! Date:_____

Type of Renovation:

_____

_____

DIY or Hire Out?

_____

_____

Priority (1–5): ✳ ✳ ✳ ✳ ✳

Accomplished! Date:_____

Spa Experiences to Indulge In

Treatment:

_____

Where to Enjoy It:

_____

Priority (1–5): ✱ ✱ ✱ ✱ ✱
Accomplished! Date: _____

Treatment:

_____

Where to Enjoy It:

_____

Priority (1–5): ✱ ✱ ✱ ✱ ✱
Accomplished! Date: _____

Treatment:

_____

Where to Enjoy It:

_____

Priority (1–5): ✱ ✱ ✱ ✱ ✱
Accomplished! Date: _____

Treatment:

_____

Where to Enjoy It:

_____

Priority (1–5): ✱ ✱ ✱ ✱ ✱
Accomplished! Date: _____

Treatment:

_____

Where to Enjoy It:

_____

Priority (1–5): ✱ ✱ ✱ ✱ ✱
Accomplished! Date: _____

Treatment:

_____

Where to Enjoy It:

_____

Priority (1–5): ✱ ✱ ✱ ✱ ✱
Accomplished! Date: _____

Treatment:

_____

Where to Enjoy It:

_____

Priority (1–5): ✱ ✱ ✱ ✱ ✱
Accomplished! Date: _____

Treatment:

_____

Where to Enjoy It:

_____

Priority (1–5): ✱ ✱ ✱ ✱ ✱
Accomplished! Date: _____

Sports to Try

Sport:
_____

Where to Learn It:
_____

Priority (1–5): ✷ ✷ ✷ ✷ ✷
Accomplished! Date: _____

Sport:
_____

Where to Learn It:
_____

Priority (1–5): ✷ ✷ ✷ ✷ ✷
Accomplished! Date: _____

Sport:
_____

Where to Learn It:
_____

Priority (1–5): ✷ ✷ ✷ ✷ ✷
Accomplished! Date: _____

Sport:
_____

Where to Learn It:
_____

Priority (1–5): ✷ ✷ ✷ ✷ ✷
Accomplished! Date: _____

Sport:
_____

Where to Learn It:
_____

Priority (1–5): ✷ ✷ ✷ ✷ ✷
Accomplished! Date: _____

Sport:
_____

Where to Learn It:
_____

Priority (1–5): ✷ ✷ ✷ ✷ ✷
Accomplished! Date: _____

Sport:
_____

Where to Learn It:
_____

Priority (1–5): ✷ ✷ ✷ ✷ ✷
Accomplished! Date: _____

Sport:
_____

Where to Learn It:
_____

Priority (1–5): ✷ ✷ ✷ ✷ ✷
Accomplished! Date: _____

PART 3

Big Dreams

You've figured out what's important to you, and you've created some lists with those items. Next up, it's time to plan the bigger stuff. The trips. The dream home. The educational journey. These pages are where you make your dreams a reality, with specific instructions and guides created by you, for you. Here again, there's a place to rank the importance of the experience to you (1–5) so you can figure out which of your adventures you definitely want to do and which are not as high of a priority. You may find that this ranking changes over time. That's fine—if so, just change it. Nothing's written in stone. After you accomplish your dreams, you get to reflect too, as there will be space for you to put photos and to journal all about what the experience meant to you.

Bucket List Item

Place/Adventure/Goal

_____

_____

_____

_____

_____

_____

_____

_____

_____

Details (who with, location, how
to get there, cost, etc.)

_____

_____

_____

_____

_____

_____

_____

_____

Priority (1–5): ✳ ✳ ✳ ✳ ✳   Target date: _____

Why it's important to me:

_____

_____

_____

_____

_____

_____

_____

_____

How to make it happen:

_____

_____

_____

_____

_____

_____

_____

_____

Date completed: _____

Expectation versus reality—any surprises?

_____
_____
_____
_____
_____
_____
_____
_____

_____
_____
_____   Best moments/photo
_____
_____
_____
_____
_____
_____
_____
_____
_____
_____
_____
_____

Bucket List Item

Place/Adventure/Goal

_____

_____
_____
_____
_____
_____
_____
_____
_____

Priority (1–5): ✶ ✶ ✶ ✶ ✶

Why it's important to me:

_____
_____
_____
_____
_____
_____
_____
_____

Details (who with, location, how to get there, cost, etc.)

_____
_____
_____
_____
_____
_____
_____
_____

Target date: _____

How to make it happen:

_____
_____
_____
_____
_____
_____
_____
_____

Date completed: _____

Expectation versus reality—any surprises?

_____
_____
_____
_____
_____
_____
_____
_____
_____

_____

_____   Best moments/photo

_____

_____

_____

_____

_____

_____

_____

_____

_____

_____

_____

_____

Bucket List Item

Place/Adventure/Goal

_____

_____

_____

_____

_____

_____

_____

_____

Details (who with, location, how to get there, cost, etc.)

_____

_____

_____

_____

_____

_____

_____

_____

Priority (1–5): ✳ ✳ ✳ ✳ ✳   Target date: _____

Why it's important to me:

_____

_____

_____

_____

_____

_____

_____

How to make it happen:

_____

_____

_____

_____

_____

_____

_____

Date completed: _____

Expectation versus reality—any surprises?

_____

_____

_____

_____

_____

_____

_____

_____

_____

_____   Best moments/photo

_____

_____

_____

_____

_____

_____

_____

_____

_____

_____

_____

_____

Bucket List Item

Place/Adventure/Goal

_____

_____

_____

_____

_____

_____

_____

_____

Details (who with, location, how to get there, cost, etc.)

_____

_____

_____

_____

_____

_____

_____

_____

Priority (1–5): ✳ ✳ ✳ ✳ ✳   Target date: _____

Why it's important to me:

_____

_____

_____

_____

_____

_____

_____

How to make it happen:

_____

_____

_____

_____

_____

_____

_____

Date completed: _____

Expectation versus reality—any surprises?

_____

_____

_____

_____

_____

_____

_____

_____

_____

_____

_____   Best moments/photo

_____

_____

_____

_____

_____

_____

_____

_____

_____

_____

_____

_____

Bucket List Item

Place/Adventure/Goal

_____

_____

_____

_____

_____

_____

_____

_____

Details (who with, location, how to get there, cost, etc.)

_____

_____

_____

_____

_____

_____

_____

Priority (1–5): ✳ ✳ ✳ ✳ ✳   Target date: _____

Why it's important to me:

_____

_____

_____

_____

_____

_____

_____

_____

How to make it happen:

_____

_____

_____

_____

_____

_____

_____

_____

Date completed: _____

Expectation versus reality—any surprises?

_____

_____

_____

_____

_____

_____

_____

_____

_____

_____   Best moments/photo

_____

_____

_____

_____

_____

_____

_____

_____

_____

_____

Bucket List Item

Place/Adventure/Goal

_____

_____

_____

_____

_____

_____

_____

_____

_____

Details (who with, location, how to get there, cost, etc.)

_____

_____

_____

_____

_____

_____

_____

_____

Priority (1–5): ✳ ✳ ✳ ✳ ✳   Target date: _____

Why it's important to me:

_____

_____

_____

_____

_____

_____

_____

_____

How to make it happen:

_____

_____

_____

_____

_____

_____

_____

_____

Date completed: _____

Expectation versus reality—any surprises?

_____

_____

_____

_____

_____

_____

_____

_____

_____

_____   Best moments/photo

_____

_____

_____

_____

_____

_____

_____

_____

_____

_____

_____

Bucket List Item

Place/Adventure/Goal

_____

_____

_____

_____

_____

_____

_____

_____

_____

Details (who with, location, how to get there, cost, etc.)

_____

_____

_____

_____

_____

_____

_____

_____

Priority (1–5): ✳ ✳ ✳ ✳ ✳

Target date: _____

Why it's important to me:

_____

_____

_____

_____

_____

_____

_____

_____

How to make it happen:

_____

_____

_____

_____

_____

_____

_____

_____

Date completed: _____

Expectation versus reality—any surprises?

_____
_____
_____
_____
_____
_____
_____
_____

Best moments/photo

_____
_____
_____
_____
_____
_____
_____
_____
_____
_____
_____
_____
_____

Bucket List Item

Place/Adventure/Goal

_____

_____

_____

_____

_____

_____

_____

_____

_____

Details (who with, location, how to get there, cost, etc.)

_____

_____

_____

_____

_____

_____

_____

_____

Priority (1–5): ✳ ✳ ✳ ✳ ✳   Target date: _____

Why it's important to me:

_____

_____

_____

_____

_____

_____

_____

_____

How to make it happen:

_____

_____

_____

_____

_____

_____

_____

_____

Date completed: _____

Expectation versus reality—any surprises?

_____

_____

_____

_____

_____

_____

_____

_____

_____

_____   Best moments/photo

_____

_____

_____

_____

_____

_____

_____

_____

_____

_____

_____

Bucket List Item

Place/Adventure/Goal

_____

_____

_____

_____

_____

_____

_____

_____

_____

Details (who with, location, how to get there, cost, etc.)

_____

_____

_____

_____

_____

_____

_____

_____

Priority (1–5): ✳ ✳ ✳ ✳ ✳

Target date: _____

Why it's important to me:

_____

_____

_____

_____

_____

_____

_____

_____

How to make it happen:

_____

_____

_____

_____

_____

_____

_____

_____

Date completed: _____

Expectation versus reality—any surprises?

_____

_____

_____

_____

_____

_____

_____

_____

_____

_____   Best moments/photo

_____

_____

_____

_____

_____

_____

_____

_____

_____

_____

_____

_____

Bucket List Item

Place/Adventure/Goal

_____

_____

_____

_____

_____

_____

_____

_____

_____

Details (who with, location, how to get there, cost, etc.)

_____

_____

_____

_____

_____

_____

_____

_____

_____

Priority (1–5): ✳ ✳ ✳ ✳ ✳   Target date: _____

Why it's important to me:

_____

_____

_____

_____

_____

_____

_____

_____

How to make it happen:

_____

_____

_____

_____

_____

_____

_____

_____

Date completed: _____

Expectation versus reality—any surprises?

_____

_____

_____

_____

_____

_____

_____

_____

_____

_____   Best moments/photo

_____

_____

_____

_____

_____

_____

_____

_____

_____

_____

_____

_____

Bucket List Item

Place/Adventure/Goal

_____

_____

_____

_____

_____

_____

_____

_____

_____

Details (who with, location, how to get there, cost, etc.)

_____

_____

_____

_____

_____

_____

_____

_____

Priority (1–5): ✳ ✳ ✳ ✳ ✳   Target date: _____

Why it's important to me:

_____

_____

_____

_____

_____

_____

_____

How to make it happen:

_____

_____

_____

_____

_____

_____

_____

Date completed: _____

Expectation versus reality—any surprises?

_____

_____

_____

_____

_____

_____

_____

_____

_____   Best moments/photo

_____

_____

_____

_____

_____

_____

_____

_____

_____

_____

_____

_____

Bucket List Item

Place/Adventure/Goal

_____

_____

_____

_____

_____

_____

_____

_____

Details (who with, location, how to get there, cost, etc.)

_____

_____

_____

_____

_____

_____

_____

_____

Priority (1–5): ✴ ✴ ✴ ✴ ✴   Target date: _____

Why it's important to me:

_____

_____

_____

_____

_____

_____

_____

How to make it happen:

_____

_____

_____

_____

_____

_____

_____

Date completed: _____

Expectation versus reality—any surprises?

_____
_____
_____
_____
_____
_____
_____
_____
_____

Best moments/photo

_____
_____
_____
_____
_____
_____
_____
_____
_____
_____
_____

Bucket List Item

Place/Adventure/Goal

_____

_____

_____

_____

_____

_____

_____

_____

_____

_____

Details (who with, location, how to get there, cost, etc.)

_____

_____

_____

_____

_____

_____

_____

_____

_____

Priority (1–5): ✳ ✳ ✳ ✳ ✳   Target date: _____

Why it's important to me:

_____

_____

_____

_____

_____

_____

_____

_____

How to make it happen:

_____

_____

_____

_____

_____

_____

_____

_____

Date completed: _____

Expectation versus reality—any surprises?

_____
_____
_____
_____
_____
_____
_____
_____
_____
_____

Best moments/photo

_____
_____
_____
_____
_____
_____
_____
_____
_____
_____
_____

Bucket List Item

Place/Adventure/Goal

_____

_____

_____

_____

_____

_____

_____

_____

Details (who with, location, how to get there, cost, etc.)

_____

_____

_____

_____

_____

_____

_____

Priority (1–5): ✳ ✳ ✳ ✳ ✳   Target date: _____

Why it's important to me:

_____

_____

_____

_____

_____

_____

_____

How to make it happen:

_____

_____

_____

_____

_____

_____

_____

Date completed: _____

Expectation versus reality—any surprises?

_____

_____

_____

_____

_____

_____

_____

_____

_____

_____   Best moments/photo

_____

_____

_____

_____

_____

_____

_____

_____

_____

_____

_____

_____

_____

Bucket List Item

Place/Adventure/Goal

_____

_____

_____

_____

_____

_____

_____

_____

_____

Details (who with, location, how to get there, cost, etc.)

_____

_____

_____

_____

_____

_____

_____

_____

Priority (1–5): ✳ ✳ ✳ ✳ ✳   Target date: _____

Why it's important to me:

_____

_____

_____

_____

_____

_____

_____

_____

How to make it happen:

_____

_____

_____

_____

_____

_____

_____

Date completed: _____

Expectation versus reality—any surprises?

_____

_____

_____

_____

_____

_____

_____

_____

_____

_____   ┌ ─ ─ ─ ─ ─ ─ ─ ─ ─ ─ ┐

_____   Best moments/photo

_____

_____

_____

_____

_____

_____

_____

_____

_____

_____   └ ─ ─ ─ ─ ─ ─ ─ ─ ─ ─ ┘

_____

Bucket List Item

Place/Adventure/Goal

_____

_____

_____

_____

_____

_____

_____

_____

_____

Details (who with, location, how to get there, cost, etc.)

_____

_____

_____

_____

_____

_____

_____

_____

Priority (1–5): ✷ ✷ ✷ ✷ ✷

Target date: _____

Why it's important to me:

_____

_____

_____

_____

_____

_____

_____

_____

How to make it happen:

_____

_____

_____

_____

_____

_____

_____

_____

Date completed: _____

Expectation versus reality—any surprises?

_____
_____
_____
_____
_____
_____
_____

_____   ┌ ─ ─ ─ ─ ─ ─ ┐
_____   │
_____   │   Best moments/photo
_____   │
_____   │
_____   │
_____   │
_____   │
_____   │
_____   │
_____   │
_____   │
_____   │
_____   └ ─ ─ ─ ─ ─ ─ ┘

Bucket List Item

Place/Adventure/Goal

_____

_____

_____

_____

_____

_____

_____

_____

Details (who with, location, how
to get there, cost, etc.)

_____

_____

_____

_____

_____

_____

_____

_____

Priority (1–5): ✳ ✳ ✳ ✳ ✳

Target date: _____

Why it's important to me:

_____

_____

_____

_____

_____

_____

_____

_____

How to make it happen:

_____

_____

_____

_____

_____

_____

_____

_____

Date completed: _____

Expectation versus reality—any surprises?

_____

_____

_____

_____

_____

_____

_____

_____

_____

_____

_____   Best moments/photo

_____

_____

_____

_____

_____

_____

_____

_____

_____

_____

Bucket List Item

Place/Adventure/Goal

_____

_____

_____

_____

_____

_____

_____

_____

_____

Details (who with, location, how to get there, cost, etc.)

_____

_____

_____

_____

_____

_____

_____

_____

Priority (1–5): ✦ ✦ ✦ ✦ ✦

Target date: _____

Why it's important to me:

_____

_____

_____

_____

_____

_____

_____

_____

How to make it happen:

_____

_____

_____

_____

_____

_____

_____

_____

Date completed: _____

Expectation versus reality—any surprises?

_____

_____

_____

_____

_____

_____

_____

_____

_____   Best moments/photo

_____

_____

_____

_____

_____

_____

_____

_____

_____

_____

_____

_____

Bucket List Item

Place/Adventure/Goal

_____

_____

_____

_____

_____

_____

_____

_____

_____

Details (who with, location, how
to get there, cost, etc.)

_____

_____

_____

_____

_____

_____

_____

_____

Priority (1–5): ✳ ✳ ✳ ✳ ✳   Target date: _____

Why it's important to me:

_____

_____

_____

_____

_____

_____

_____

_____

How to make it happen:

_____

_____

_____

_____

_____

_____

_____

_____

Date completed: _____

Expectation versus reality—any surprises?

_____

_____

_____

_____

_____

_____

_____

_____

_____

_____

_____ Best moments/photo

_____

_____

_____

_____

_____

_____

_____

_____

_____

_____

Bucket List Item

Place/Adventure/Goal

_____

_____

_____

_____

_____

_____

_____

_____

_____

Details (who with, location, how to get there, cost, etc.)

_____

_____

_____

_____

_____

_____

_____

_____

Priority (1–5): ✳ ✳ ✳ ✳ ✳   Target date: _____

Why it's important to me:

_____

_____

_____

_____

_____

_____

_____

How to make it happen:

_____

_____

_____

_____

_____

_____

Date completed: _____

Expectation versus reality—any surprises?

_____

_____

_____

_____

_____

_____

_____

_____

_____

_____

_____   Best moments/photo

_____

_____

_____

_____

_____

_____

_____

_____

_____

_____

_____

Bucket List Item

Place/Adventure/Goal

_____

_____

_____

_____

_____

_____

_____

_____

_____

_____

Details (who with, location, how to get there, cost, etc.)

_____

_____

_____

_____

_____

_____

_____

_____

_____

Priority (1–5): ✳ ✳ ✳ ✳ ✳

Target date: _____

Why it's important to me:

_____

_____

_____

_____

_____

_____

_____

_____

How to make it happen:

_____

_____

_____

_____

_____

_____

_____

_____

Date completed: _____

Expectation versus reality—any surprises?

_____

_____

_____

_____

_____

_____

_____

_____

_____

_____

_____   Best moments/photo

_____

_____

_____

_____

_____

_____

_____

_____

_____

_____

_____

_____

Bucket List Item

Place/Adventure/Goal

_____

_____

_____

_____

_____

_____

_____

_____

_____

Details (who with, location, how to get there, cost, etc.)

_____

_____

_____

_____

_____

_____

_____

_____

Priority (1–5): ✳ ✳ ✳ ✳ ✳   Target date: _____

Why it's important to me:

_____

_____

_____

_____

_____

_____

_____

_____

How to make it happen:

_____

_____

_____

_____

_____

_____

_____

_____

Date completed: _____

Expectation versus reality—any surprises?

_____

_____

_____

_____

_____

_____

_____

_____

_____

_____

_____   Best moments/photo

_____

_____

_____

_____

_____

_____

_____

_____

_____

_____

_____

Bucket List Item

Place/Adventure/Goal

_____

_____

_____

_____

_____

_____

_____

_____

_____

Details (who with, location, how to get there, cost, etc.)

_____

_____

_____

_____

_____

_____

_____

_____

Priority (1–5): ✳ ✳ ✳ ✳ ✳   Target date: _____

Why it's important to me:

_____

_____

_____

_____

_____

_____

_____

How to make it happen:

_____

_____

_____

_____

_____

_____

_____

_____

Date completed: _____

Expectation versus reality—any surprises?

_____

_____

_____

_____

_____

_____

_____

_____

_____

_____

_____   Best moments/photo

_____

_____

_____

_____

_____

_____

_____

_____

_____

_____

_____

Bucket List Item

Place/Adventure/Goal

_____

_____

_____

_____

_____

_____

_____

_____

_____

Details (who with, location, how to get there, cost, etc.)

_____

_____

_____

_____

_____

_____

_____

_____

Priority (1–5): ✳ ✳ ✳ ✳ ✳

Target date: _____

Why it's important to me:

_____

_____

_____

_____

_____

_____

_____

How to make it happen:

_____

_____

_____

_____

_____

_____

_____

Date completed: _____

Expectation versus reality—any surprises?

_____

_____

_____

_____

_____

_____

_____

_____

_____

_____

Best moments/photo

_____

_____

_____

_____

_____

_____

_____

_____

_____

_____

_____

Bucket List Item

Place/Adventure/Goal

_____

_____

_____

_____

_____

_____

_____

_____

_____

Details (who with, location, how to get there, cost, etc.)

_____

_____

_____

_____

_____

_____

_____

_____

Priority (1–5): ✳ ✳ ✳ ✳ ✳

Target date: _____

Why it's important to me:

_____

_____

_____

_____

_____

_____

_____

_____

How to make it happen:

_____

_____

_____

_____

_____

_____

_____

_____

Date completed: _____

Expectation versus reality—any surprises?

_____
_____
_____
_____
_____
_____
_____
_____

_____   ┌ ─ ─ ─ ─ ─ ─ ─ ┐
_____
_____   Best moments/photo
_____
_____
_____
_____
_____
_____
_____
_____
_____
_____
_____
_____   └ ─ ─ ─ ─ ─ ─ ─ ┘

Bucket List Item

Place/Adventure/Goal

_____
_____
_____
_____
_____
_____
_____
_____
_____

Details (who with, location, how to get there, cost, etc.)

_____
_____
_____
_____
_____
_____
_____
_____
_____

Priority (1–5): ✳ ✳ ✳ ✳ ✳   Target date: _____

Why it's important to me:

_____
_____
_____
_____
_____
_____
_____
_____

How to make it happen:

_____
_____
_____
_____
_____
_____
_____
_____

Date completed: _____

Expectation versus reality—any surprises?

_____

_____

_____

_____

_____

_____

_____

_____

_____

_____

_____

_____

_____

_____

_____

_____

_____

_____

_____

_____

_____

_____

Best moments/photo

Bucket List Item

Place/Adventure/Goal

_____

_____

_____

_____

_____

_____

_____

_____

_____

Details (who with, location, how to get there, cost, etc.)

_____

_____

_____

_____

_____

_____

_____

_____

Priority (1–5): ✳ ✳ ✳ ✳ ✳

Target date: _____

Why it's important to me:

_____

_____

_____

_____

_____

_____

_____

_____

How to make it happen:

_____

_____

_____

_____

_____

_____

_____

_____

Date completed: _____

Expectation versus reality—any surprises?

_____

_____

_____

_____

_____

_____

_____

_____

_____   Best moments/photo

_____

_____

_____

_____

_____

_____

_____

_____

_____

_____

_____

_____

Bucket List Item

Place/Adventure/Goal

_____

_____
_____
_____
_____
_____
_____
_____
_____

Details (who with, location, how
to get there, cost, etc.)

_____
_____
_____
_____
_____
_____
_____
_____

Priority (1–5): ✳ ✳ ✳ ✳ ✳   Target date: _____

Why it's important to me:

_____
_____
_____
_____
_____
_____
_____

How to make it happen:

_____
_____
_____
_____
_____
_____
_____

Date completed: _____

Expectation versus reality—any surprises?

_____

_____

_____

_____

_____

_____

_____

_____

_____

_____

_____   Best moments/photo

_____

_____

_____

_____

_____

_____

_____

_____

_____

_____

_____

_____

_____

Bucket List Item

Place/Adventure/Goal

_____

_____

_____

_____

_____

_____

_____

_____

_____

Details (who with, location, how to get there, cost, etc.)

_____

_____

_____

_____

_____

_____

_____

_____

Priority (1–5): ✳ ✳ ✳ ✳ ✳

Target date: _____

Why it's important to me:

_____

_____

_____

_____

_____

_____

_____

_____

How to make it happen:

_____

_____

_____

_____

_____

_____

_____

_____

Date completed: _____

Expectation versus reality—any surprises?

_____

_____

_____

_____

_____

_____

_____

_____

_____

_____

_____   Best moments/photo

_____

_____

_____

_____

_____

_____

_____

_____

_____

_____

Bucket List Item

Place/Adventure/Goal

_____

_____

_____

_____

_____

_____

_____

_____

_____

Details (who with, location, how to get there, cost, etc.)

_____

_____

_____

_____

_____

_____

_____

_____

Priority (1–5): ✳ ✳ ✳ ✳ ✳   Target date: _____

Why it's important to me:

_____

_____

_____

_____

_____

_____

_____

_____

How to make it happen:

_____

_____

_____

_____

_____

_____

_____

_____

Date completed: _____

Expectation versus reality—any surprises?

_____
_____
_____
_____
_____
_____
_____
_____
_____

_____
_____   Best moments/photo
_____
_____
_____
_____
_____
_____
_____
_____
_____
_____

Bucket List Item

Place/Adventure/Goal

_____

_____

_____

_____

_____

_____

_____

_____

_____

Details (who with, location, how to get there, cost, etc.)

_____

_____

_____

_____

_____

_____

_____

_____

_____

Priority (1–5): ✳ ✳ ✳ ✳ ✳   Target date: _____

Why it's important to me:

_____

_____

_____

_____

_____

_____

_____

How to make it happen:

_____

_____

_____

_____

_____

_____

_____

Date completed: _____

Expectation versus reality—any surprises?

_____

_____

_____

_____

_____

_____

_____

_____

_____

_____   Best moments/photo

_____

_____

_____

_____

_____

_____

_____

_____

_____

_____

_____

_____

Bucket List Item

Place/Adventure/Goal

_____

_____

_____

_____

_____

_____

_____

_____

_____

Details (who with, location, how to get there, cost, etc.)

_____

_____

_____

_____

_____

_____

_____

_____

_____

Priority (1–5): ✳ ✳ ✳ ✳ ✳

Target date: _____

Why it's important to me:

_____

_____

_____

_____

_____

_____

_____

_____

How to make it happen:

_____

_____

_____

_____

_____

_____

_____

_____

Date completed: _____

Expectation versus reality—any surprises?

_____

_____

_____

_____

_____

_____

_____

_____

_____

_____

_____   Best moments/photo

_____

_____

_____

_____

_____

_____

_____

_____

_____

_____

_____

_____

_____

Bucket List Item

Place/Adventure/Goal

_____

_____

_____

_____

_____

_____

_____

_____

_____

Details (who with, location, how to get there, cost, etc.)

_____

_____

_____

_____

_____

_____

_____

_____

_____

Priority (1–5): ✳ ✳ ✳ ✳ ✳   Target date: _____

Why it's important to me:

_____

_____

_____

_____

_____

_____

_____

_____

How to make it happen:

_____

_____

_____

_____

_____

_____

_____

_____

Date completed: _____

Expectation versus reality—any surprises?

_____

_____

_____

_____

_____

_____

_____

_____

_____   Best moments/photo

_____

_____

_____

_____

_____

_____

_____

_____

_____

_____

_____

Bucket List Item

Place/Adventure/Goal

_____
_____
_____
_____
_____
_____
_____
_____
_____

Details (who with, location, how to get there, cost, etc.)

_____
_____
_____
_____
_____
_____
_____
_____

Priority (1–5): ✳ ✳ ✳ ✳ ✳

Target date: _____

Why it's important to me:

_____
_____
_____
_____
_____
_____
_____
_____

How to make it happen:

_____
_____
_____
_____
_____
_____
_____
_____

Date completed: _____

Expectation versus reality—any surprises?

_____

_____

_____

_____

_____

_____

_____

_____

_____

_____   Best moments/photo

_____

_____

_____

_____

_____

_____

_____

_____

_____

_____

_____

_____

_____

Bucket List Item

Place/Adventure/Goal

_____

_____

_____

_____

_____

_____

_____

_____

_____

Details (who with, location, how to get there, cost, etc.)

_____

_____

_____

_____

_____

_____

_____

_____

_____

Priority (1–5): ✳ ✳ ✳ ✳ ✳

Target date: _____

Why it's important to me:

_____

_____

_____

_____

_____

_____

_____

How to make it happen:

_____

_____

_____

_____

_____

_____

_____

Date completed: _____

Expectation versus reality—any surprises?

_____
_____
_____
_____
_____
_____
_____
_____
_____

_____   Best moments/photo
_____
_____
_____
_____
_____
_____
_____
_____
_____
_____
_____
_____
_____

Bucket List Item

Place/Adventure/Goal

_____

_____

_____

_____

_____

_____

_____

_____

_____

Details (who with, location, how
to get there, cost, etc.)

_____

_____

_____

_____

_____

_____

_____

_____

Priority (1–5): ✳ ✳ ✳ ✳ ✳   Target date: _____

Why it's important to me:

_____

_____

_____

_____

_____

_____

_____

_____

How to make it happen:

_____

_____

_____

_____

_____

_____

_____

_____

Date completed: _____

Expectation versus reality—any surprises?

_____

_____

_____

_____

_____

_____

_____

_____

_____

_____

_____   Best moments/photo

_____

_____

_____

_____

_____

_____

_____

_____

_____

_____

_____

_____

Bucket List Item

Place/Adventure/Goal

_____

_____

_____

_____

_____

_____

_____

_____

_____

Details (who with, location, how to get there, cost, etc.)

_____

_____

_____

_____

_____

_____

_____

_____

_____

Priority (1–5): ✴ ✴ ✴ ✴ ✴

Target date: _____

Why it's important to me:

_____

_____

_____

_____

_____

_____

_____

How to make it happen:

_____

_____

_____

_____

_____

_____

_____

Date completed: _____

Expectation versus reality—any surprises?

_____

_____

_____

_____

_____

_____

_____

_____

_____

_____

_____   Best moments/photo

_____

_____

_____

_____

_____

_____

_____

_____

_____

_____

Bucket List Item

Place/Adventure/Goal

_____

_____

_____

_____

_____

_____

_____

_____

Details (who with, location, how
to get there, cost, etc.)

_____

_____

_____

_____

_____

_____

_____

_____

Priority (1–5): ✳ ✳ ✳ ✳ ✳   Target date: _____

Why it's important to me:

_____

_____

_____

_____

_____

_____

_____

How to make it happen:

_____

_____

_____

_____

_____

_____

_____

Date completed: _____

Expectation versus reality—any surprises?

_____

_____

_____

_____

_____

_____

_____

_____

_____

_____

_____

_____

_____

_____

_____

_____

_____

_____

_____

_____

_____

Best moments/photo

Bucket List Item

Place/Adventure/Goal

Details (who with, location, how
to get there, cost, etc.)

_____

Priority (1–5): ✳ ✳ ✳ ✳ ✳   Target date: _____

Why it's important to me: How to make it happen:

Date completed: _____

Expectation versus reality—any surprises?

_____

_____

_____

_____

_____

_____

_____

_____

_____

_____

_____   Best moments/photo

_____

_____

_____

_____

_____

_____

_____

_____

_____

_____

_____

Bucket List Item

Place/Adventure/Goal

_____

_____

_____

_____

_____

_____

_____

_____

_____

Details (who with, location, how to get there, cost, etc.)

_____

_____

_____

_____

_____

_____

_____

_____

Priority (1–5): ✳ ✳ ✳ ✳ ✳   Target date: _____

Why it's important to me:

_____

_____

_____

_____

_____

_____

_____

_____

How to make it happen:

_____

_____

_____

_____

_____

_____

_____

_____

Date completed: _____

Expectation versus reality—any surprises?

_____

_____

_____

_____

_____

_____

_____

_____

_____

Best moments/photo

_____

_____

_____

_____

_____

_____

_____

_____

_____

Bucket List Item

Place/Adventure/Goal

_____

_____

_____

_____

_____

_____

_____

_____

Details (who with, location, how to get there, cost, etc.)

_____

_____

_____

_____

_____

_____

_____

Priority (1–5): ✳ ✳ ✳ ✳ ✳   Target date: _____

Why it's important to me:

_____

_____

_____

_____

_____

_____

_____

How to make it happen:

_____

_____

_____

_____

_____

_____

_____

Date completed: _____

Expectation versus reality—any surprises?

_____
_____
_____
_____
_____
_____
_____
_____
_____

_____
_____   Best moments/photo
_____
_____
_____
_____
_____
_____
_____
_____
_____
_____
_____
_____
_____
_____

Bucket List Item

Place/Adventure/Goal

_____

_____

_____

_____

_____

_____

_____

_____

_____

Details (who with, location, how to get there, cost, etc.)

_____

_____

_____

_____

_____

_____

_____

_____

Priority (1–5): ✳ ✳ ✳ ✳ ✳   Target date: _____

Why it's important to me:

_____

_____

_____

_____

_____

_____

_____

How to make it happen:

_____

_____

_____

_____

_____

_____

_____

Date completed: _____

Expectation versus reality—any surprises?

_____
_____
_____
_____
_____
_____
_____
_____
_____
_____
_____

Best moments/photo

_____
_____
_____
_____
_____
_____
_____
_____
_____
_____
_____
_____
_____
_____

Bucket List Item

Place/Adventure/Goal

_____

_____

_____

_____

_____

_____

_____

_____

Details (who with, location, how to get there, cost, etc.)

_____

_____

_____

_____

_____

_____

_____

_____

Priority (1–5): ✳ ✳ ✳ ✳ ✳   Target date: _____

Why it's important to me:

_____

_____

_____

_____

_____

_____

_____

How to make it happen:

_____

_____

_____

_____

_____

_____

_____

Date completed: _____

Expectation versus reality—any surprises?

_____

_____

_____

_____

_____

_____

_____

_____

_____

_____   Best moments/photo

_____

_____

_____

_____

_____

_____

_____

_____

_____

_____

_____

_____

Bucket List Item

Place/Adventure/Goal

_____

_____

_____

_____

_____

_____

_____

_____

_____

Details (who with, location, how to get there, cost, etc.)

_____

_____

_____

_____

_____

_____

_____

_____

Priority (1–5): ✳ ✳ ✳ ✳ ✳   Target date: _____

Why it's important to me:

_____

_____

_____

_____

_____

_____

_____

_____

How to make it happen:

_____

_____

_____

_____

_____

_____

_____

_____

Date completed: _____

Expectation versus reality—any surprises?

_____
_____
_____
_____
_____
_____
_____
_____
_____

Best moments/photo

Bucket List Item

Place/Adventure/Goal

_____

_____

_____

_____

_____

_____

_____

_____

Details (who with, location, how to get there, cost, etc.)

_____

_____

_____

_____

_____

_____

_____

_____

Priority (1–5): ✳ ✳ ✳ ✳ ✳

Target date: _____

Why it's important to me:

_____

_____

_____

_____

_____

_____

_____

How to make it happen:

_____

_____

_____

_____

_____

_____

_____

Date completed: _____

Expectation versus reality—any surprises?

_____

_____

_____

_____

_____

_____

_____

_____

_____   Best moments/photo

_____

_____

_____

_____

_____

_____

_____

_____

_____

_____

_____

_____

Bucket List Item

Place/Adventure/Goal

_____

_____

_____

_____

_____

_____

_____

_____

_____

Details (who with, location, how to get there, cost, etc.)

_____

_____

_____

_____

_____

_____

_____

_____

Priority (1–5): ✳ ✳ ✳ ✳ ✳   Target date: _____

Why it's important to me:

_____

_____

_____

_____

_____

_____

_____

_____

How to make it happen:

_____

_____

_____

_____

_____

_____

_____

_____

Date completed: _____

Expectation versus reality—any surprises?

_____

_____

_____

_____

_____

_____

_____

_____

_____

_____   Best moments/photo

_____

_____

_____

_____

_____

_____

_____

_____

_____

_____

Bucket List Item

Place/Adventure/Goal

_____

_____

_____

_____

_____

_____

_____

_____

_____

Details (who with, location, how to get there, cost, etc.)

_____

_____

_____

_____

_____

_____

_____

_____

_____

Priority (1–5): ✳ ✳ ✳ ✳ ✳

Target date: _____

Why it's important to me:

_____

_____

_____

_____

_____

_____

_____

How to make it happen:

_____

_____

_____

_____

_____

_____

_____

Date completed: _____

Expectation versus reality—any surprises?

_____

_____

_____

_____

_____

_____

_____

_____

_____

_____   **Best moments/photo**

_____

_____

_____

_____

_____

_____

_____

_____

_____

_____

_____

Bucket List Item

Place/Adventure/Goal

_____
_____
_____
_____
_____
_____
_____
_____

Details (who with, location, how to get there, cost, etc.)

_____
_____
_____
_____
_____
_____
_____
_____

Priority (1–5): ✳ ✳ ✳ ✳ ✳   Target date: _____

Why it's important to me:

_____
_____
_____
_____
_____
_____
_____
_____

How to make it happen:

_____
_____
_____
_____
_____
_____
_____
_____

Date completed: _____

Expectation versus reality—any surprises?

_____

_____

_____

_____

_____

_____

_____

_____

_____

_____   Best moments/photo

_____

_____

_____

_____

_____

_____

_____

_____

_____

_____

_____

Bucket List Item

Place/Adventure/Goal

_____

_____

_____

_____

_____

_____

_____

_____

Details (who with, location, how to get there, cost, etc.)

_____

_____

_____

_____

_____

_____

_____

_____

Priority (1–5): ✳ ✳ ✳ ✳ ✳   Target date: _____

Why it's important to me:

_____

_____

_____

_____

_____

_____

_____

How to make it happen:

_____

_____

_____

_____

_____

_____

_____

Date completed: _____

Expectation versus reality—any surprises?

_____

_____

_____

_____

_____

_____

_____

_____

_____

_____

_____

_____   Best moments/photo

_____

_____

_____

_____

_____

_____

_____

_____

_____

_____

_____

_____

Bucket List Item

Place/Adventure/Goal

Details (who with, location, how
to get there, cost, etc.)

_____

Priority (1–5): ✴ ✴ ✴ ✴ ✴   Target date: _____

Why it's important to me:

How to make it happen:

Date completed: _____

Expectation versus reality—any surprises?

_____

_____

_____

_____

_____

_____

_____

_____

_____

_____

_____

_____

_____

_____

_____

_____

_____

_____

_____

_____

Best moments/photo

Bucket List Item

Place/Adventure/Goal

_____

_____

_____

_____

_____

_____

_____

_____

Details (who with, location, how to get there, cost, etc.)

_____

_____

_____

_____

_____

_____

_____

_____

Priority (1–5): ✷ ✷ ✷ ✷ ✷

Target date: _____

Why it's important to me:

_____

_____

_____

_____

_____

_____

_____

_____

How to make it happen:

_____

_____

_____

_____

_____

_____

_____

_____

Date completed: _____

Expectation versus reality—any surprises?

_____

_____

_____

_____

_____

_____

_____

_____

_____

_____ Best moments/photo

_____

_____

_____

_____

_____

_____

_____

_____

_____

_____

_____

_____

_____

_____

Bucket List Item

Place/Adventure/Goal

_____

_____

_____

_____

_____

_____

_____

_____

_____

Details (who with, location, how
to get there, cost, etc.)

_____

_____

_____

_____

_____

_____

_____

_____

Priority (1–5): ✳ ✳ ✳ ✳ ✳   Target date: _____

Why it's important to me:

_____

_____

_____

_____

_____

_____

_____

_____

How to make it happen:

_____

_____

_____

_____

_____

_____

_____

_____

Date completed: _____

Expectation versus reality—any surprises?

_____

_____

_____

_____

_____

_____

_____

_____

_____

_____   Best moments/photo

_____

_____

_____

_____

_____

_____

_____

_____

_____

_____

_____

_____

Bucket List Item

Place/Adventure/Goal

_____

_____

_____

_____

_____

_____

_____

_____

_____

Details (who with, location, how to get there, cost, etc.)

_____

_____

_____

_____

_____

_____

_____

_____

Priority (1–5): ✳ ✳ ✳ ✳ ✳   Target date: _____

Why it's important to me:

_____

_____

_____

_____

_____

_____

_____

How to make it happen:

_____

_____

_____

_____

_____

_____

_____

Date completed: _____

Expectation versus reality—any surprises?

_____

_____

_____

_____

_____

_____

_____

_____

_____

_____

_____   Best moments/photo

_____

_____

_____

_____

_____

_____

_____

_____

_____

_____

Bucket List Item

Place/Adventure/Goal

Details (who with, location, how to get there, cost, etc.)

_____

Priority (1–5): ✳ ✳ ✳ ✳ ✳   Target date: _____

Why it's important to me:

How to make it happen:

Date completed: _____

Expectation versus reality—any surprises?

_____
_____
_____
_____
_____
_____
_____
_____
_____
_____

_____   Best moments/photo
_____
_____
_____
_____
_____
_____
_____
_____
_____
_____
_____
_____

Bucket List Item

Place/Adventure/Goal

_____

_____

_____

_____

_____

_____

_____

_____

_____

_____

Details (who with, location, how
to get there, cost, etc.)

_____

_____

_____

_____

_____

_____

_____

_____

_____

Priority (1–5): ✳ ✳ ✳ ✳ ✳   Target date: _____

Why it's important to me:

_____

_____

_____

_____

_____

_____

_____

_____

How to make it happen:

_____

_____

_____

_____

_____

_____

_____

_____